The Care & Keeping of
YOU

The Body Book for Girls

By Valorie Lee Schaefer
Illustrated by Norm Bendell

★ American Girl®

Dear American Girl,

I am a preteen and all of a sudden growing up is becoming a big and important issue. I don't feel comfortable talking to my parents about it. I feel like it's too personal to talk to an adult about. Please help me.

Growing Up

Published by American Girl Publishing, Inc.

Questions or comments?
Call 1-800-845-0005, visit our Web site at **americangirl.com,**
or write to Customer Service, American Girl,
8400 Fairway Place, Middleton, WI 53562-0497.

Printed in the United States of America.
  11 12 13 14 15 WCR 55 54 53

All American Girl marks are trademarks of American Girl, LLC.

Editorial Development: Michelle Nowadly Watkins, Andrea Weiss
Creative Director: Kym Abrams
Managing Art Director: Marilyn Dawson
Design: Ingrid Hess
Medical Consultant: Dr. Lia Gaggino, Pediatrician

Library of Congress Cataloging-in-Publication Data
Schaefer, Valorie Lee
The care and keeping of you : the body book for girls / by Valorie Schaefer ;
illustrated by Norm Bendell.
p. cm. "American girl library."
Summary: A preteen girl's guide to basic health and hygiene—from braces to bras,
pimples to periods, hair care to healthy eating.
ISBN 978-1-56247-666-3
1. Girls—Health and hygiene—Juvenile literature. 2. Grooming for girls—Juvenile
literature. [1. Girls—Health and hygiene. 2. Grooming.] I. Bendell, Norm, ill.
II. American girl library (Middleton, Wis.) III. Title.
RA777.25.S33 1998 613'.04242—dc21   98-24817 CIP AC

This book is not intended to replace the advice of or treatment by physicians, psychologists, or other health-care professionals. It should be considered an additional resource only. Questions and concerns about mental or physical health should always be discussed with a doctor or other health-care provider.

Letter to You

When you were little, your parents took care of you. Now that you're **older,** you're taking over a lot of that **responsibility,** and it's not always easy to know what to do or how to ask for help. It's a struggle for any girl to ask **questions** when she's dying of embarrassment and digging for the right words to use.

So what can you do? For starters, you need to get **information.** The more you know about your body, the less confusing and embarrassing **growing up** will seem—and the easier it will be to talk about.

We hope the **head-to-toe advice** in this book will give you the words to start a conversation with your **parents** or other adults you trust. Your parents were there for you when you were little, and they can still be there for you now. If you **speak up,** no matter how awkward you feel, your **confidence** and **spirit** will grow right along with your body!

Your friends at *American Girl*

Contents

9 yrs.

7 yrs

5 yrs.

3 yrs

1 yr.

Body Basics

With your body on the brink of some pretty big **changes,** it's time to start taking control of your **health** and **well-being.** This section introduces you to the **basic facts** about **puberty** and reminds you to take care of yourself, inside *and* out.

The Basic Facts

Taking care of your body is a lifelong job. And it's more important than ever right now, while you're going through big changes.

Are you the shortest girl in your class, or do you tower above everyone, including the boys? All of that could change in the very near future!

The Changes Ahead

Puberty is a special time of growth and change. *Everybody* goes through it. It begins for most girls between the ages of 8 and 13, and it ends when your body has reached its adult height and size, around ages 15 to 17.

During puberty you'll grow up and out, and not all parts will grow at the same rate. At times you may look and feel like a puppy whose paws are too big for its body! You'll notice changes in your skin, hair, breasts, and other parts of your body. And you'll experience new emotions, too. All of these changes are caused by *hormones,* chemicals your body produces to change you from a young girl to a woman.

Get Informed

You may be eager for your body to get growing, or you may be worried about the changes ahead. But the more you know about your body, the less surprised you'll be. So get the facts. Reading books like this one is a great start. You'll find answers to questions you may have never even thought of!

But no book is a substitute for talking to your parents, your doctor, or other adults you trust—people whose job is to take care of you. No question is too silly or too embarrassing to ask. Remember, the grown-ups in your life were once your age, too, and have experience and wisdom to share with you.

Celebrate YOU

Remember that your body is a work in progress. Try not to focus on what it *looks like*. Instead, think about all the great things your body can *do*.

You may feel like you don't have any control over your growing body. Not true! You *are* the boss when it comes to taking care of these basics.

Pay Attention

Your body is talking to you. Can you hear it? Learn to tune in to your body and hear its warnings. If your body says it's thirsty, drink more water. If your body is tired, give it a rest.

Keep Clean

All that hard work your body's doing to grow up means you'll need to bathe or shower more often, especially if you're active in sweaty sports.

Exercise

You don't have to be an Olympic athlete to be healthy. Just put down that video game, get off the couch, and get moving! Skate to a friend's house or dance to your favorite music. The busier you keep your body, the better you'll feel.

Just Don't

No girl can look and feel her best with cigarette smoke, alcohol, or drugs in her body. Though drinking and smoking may seem "grown-up," the truth is, they're bad for your health. And drugs can destroy your family and future. A smart girl turns her back and walks away from so-called friends who put pressure on her to "just try it."

PRIVATE

Your body is yours and *yours alone.* You have the right to protect it and keep it private from anyone—family, friend, or stranger. If any person touches you in a way that makes you feel uncomfortable, tell an adult you trust *immediately.* You should never keep a secret that is harmful to you or protect anyone who is hurting you.

If you feel good about yourself on the inside, you'll sparkle on the outside!

Most images of women you see on TV just aren't realistic. Look around. *Real* women's bodies look like your mom's, your teacher's, your next-door neighbor's.

Compare? No Fair!

It's tempting to compare yourself to the girls you see on TV and in magazines and movies. But hold on! Is it fair to measure yourself against made-in-Hollywood images created by makeup artists and photo wizards? No way! You don't need to measure yourself against anyone at all, including friends or other girls at school. You're you—a one-of-a-kind original—and you're beautiful in your own unique way.

It Isn't a Race

A girl's body changes to a woman's body gradually, not overnight. Each girl develops at her own rate. Even sisters don't develop at the same rate. And it's important to remember that growing up isn't a race. There are no prizes for being the first—or last—girl to lose all her baby teeth or to wear a bra. Trust that your body will do all the right things at the time that is right for you.

What's on the Inside

The most attractive girl in the room isn't the girl with the thinnest waist or the fairest face. It's the girl who brims with self-confidence. She's the one who stands head and shoulders above the crowd. That girl can be you. It all starts with a positive attitude.

To have a positive attitude, try to see yourself as a whole person shining through your features. Focus on what's best about you and refuse to hunt for negatives. Don't doubt yourself—be proud of yourself for doing your best.

Kindness Counts

As your body is growing and changing, be kind to yourself. And remember to be kind to other girls, too. They want to feel good about themselves, just like you do.

Heads Up!

Let's take it from the top, with tips for handling

your **hair,** sound advice on **ears,** and bright

tips for bright **eyes.** Learn how a healthy

mouth makes for a great grin. Brush up on

tooth, gum, and **braces** basics. Finally, get

the scoop on the skin you're in so you can put

your best **face** forward!

Hair Care

Start your everyday grooming routine right at the top with clean, shiny, freshly combed hair.

Do Keep It Clean

As you get older, your hair may get more oily. Keep it clean by washing it regularly. For most girls this means several times a week. If you're an active athlete, or if you have very oily hair, you may want to wash it every day. Use a mild shampoo that's made for your hair type. If your hair tangles easily, use a conditioner to smooth it out.

Do De-chlorinate

If you're a swimmer, rinse the pool water out of your hair after every dip. Chlorine can be very drying, and other chemicals can turn blond hair green. You can buy special shampoos made for swimmers, but regular shampoo often works just as well.

Do Wash Tools

Make sure your brushes and combs are as squeaky-clean as your hair. About once a week, give them a swish in warm, soapy water—you can use shampoo or even mild dish detergent. Rinse thoroughly.

Don't Mangle Tangles

While your hair is still wet, use a wide-tooth comb to detangle small sections. Start with the ends first and work your way up. If you hit a rough spot, don't yank! Gently work the comb through your hair.

Do Use the Right Tools

Some hair care tools can damage your hair and scalp. Choose a brush with a rubber base and round-tipped bristles. Never use a brush on wet hair, which is weaker than dry hair—the brush stretches the hair out and can cause it to break. Use a wide-tooth comb instead.

Don't Share

Sharing is a good thing, except when it comes to hair tools. Don't borrow combs and brushes from friends or family members, and don't lend them yours. It isn't stingy—it's good hygiene.

Don't Overheat

Blow-dryers, straightening irons, and curling irons can really dry out your hair. If possible, let your hair dry naturally. If you use a blow-dryer, use the warm or cool setting. Don't use straightening irons and curling irons every day—save them for special occasions.

17

Hair Scare!

When hair-raising horrors happen to you, here's how to handle them.

Getting Gum Out

Uh-oh! Somehow you've managed to get a big, juicy wad of gum in your hair. Before you reach for the scissors, try this age-old trick. Spread a glob of peanut butter on the gum. Work the peanut butter through your hair until the gum comes out. The peanut butter will wash out with a regular shampoo.

Greasy Hair

During puberty, your oil glands get more active. For some girls this means greasy hair. If the roots of your hair look oily almost every day, you may have to shampoo more often.

Dandruff!

Does your scalp feel dry and itchy? Are your shoulders covered with flakes of skin, making your dark-colored shirts look like they're sprinkled with snow? You may have a case of *dandruff,* a very common condition that's easy to treat. Try a dandruff shampoo from the drugstore. If drugstore shampoos don't work, ask your doctor for something stronger.

Hair products such as mousse, sprays, and gels can cause flakes and itching from buildup. Shampoo regularly to remove the buildup.

EEK—a Louse!

Head lice are a common problem among schoolkids everywhere. These tiny wingless parasites thrive in thickets of human hair. They bite the scalp, leaving tiny sores that itch like crazy. Worst of all, a single louse can lay hundreds of eggs, called *nits,* right on your head! If lice are on the loose at your school, take action to protect yourself. Don't share combs and brushes with friends. Don't swap hats, hair bands, or headphones, and don't trade pillows at sleepovers.

If you suspect unwelcome guests on your head, see your doctor or school nurse. They know a louse when they see one. Live lice are small and gray, and move around. Nits look like white grains of sand and are often found along the hairline above the neck and behind the ears. If it turns out you have lice, you can buy delousing products at the drugstore. Follow the instructions carefully to get rid of the lice completely and to keep them from coming back.

Nits "glue" themselves to hair and can be hard to get out. A special fine-tooth "nit comb" can help pick out the nits.

Ears

Ears are easy to care for. They need just a little help from you to stay healthy inside and out—so every sound you hear will be crystal clear.

Squeaky Clean

Your ears get washed every time you shampoo or shower. In most cases, that's all the cleaning they need. Shake your head to remove excess water, and use a towel, washcloth, or cotton swab to wipe off the outer part of your ears. NEVER stick a pointy object *into* your ears—not even a cotton swab. You could do serious damage to your eardrums or canals. Ear wax, that sticky yellowish stuff inside, is something you're supposed to have. Wax acts as a sort of flypaper, sticking to dirt and preventing it from traveling into your ear canal. You can, however, have too much wax. If your ears feel plugged, call your doctor to find out a safe way to get the gobs out.

Pierced Ears

If you want to get your ears pierced, go to a professional who uses clean, sterile equipment. Allow two to three months for the holes to heal before you change earrings. Clean your newly pierced ears daily with a cotton swab dipped in rubbing alcohol. Redness, itching, or oozing near the hole may be a sign of infection. If this happens, call your doctor for advice.

Headphones

It's OK to turn on the music and tune out the world, but don't turn up the volume! Over time, exposing your ears to loud noise can damage your hearing. Take this test. If someone stands next to you and can hear sound coming out of your headphones, it's too loud.

Many girls are allergic to the metals used in cheap earrings. To be safe, look for surgical steel, sterling silver, or 14-karat gold.

Swimmer's Ear

If you spend your summers at the lake or in the pool, you're a good candidate for swimmer's ear. This is an infection that occurs when bacteria in the water gets into your ear and grows, causing a painful earache. The best way to prevent swimmer's ear is to dry out the ears and disinfect the canals. Follow these steps:

1 After you swim, dry your ears thoroughly with a towel.

2 Mix 1 teaspoon rubbing alcohol with 1 teaspoon white vinegar. Put a few drops in each ear. The alcohol helps dry out the ear, and the vinegar kills bacteria.

3 If you have ear pain, especially when you tug on your ear, see a doctor.

Eyes

It's a good idea to have your vision checked every year at school or your doctor's office. If you have trouble seeing things far away, such as a blackboard, you may be *nearsighted*. If you have trouble reading up close, you may be *farsighted*.

Be on the Lookout

Many girls don't notice problems with their eyesight until they have to do a lot of reading or looking at the chalkboard in school. This is often between third and fifth grades. You may need glasses if you have:

❑ headaches while or after you've been reading.
❑ trouble seeing objects at a distance or up close.
❑ double vision *not* caused by just crossing your eyes.

Eye Exams

If you're having difficulty with your eyes, have them checked by an eye-care professional. Even if you aren't having problems, doctors say you should have an exam by the time you've begun to read. It's important to check for early signs of disease. At the exam, you'll be asked to read a special chart up close and at a distance. The doctor will look at your eyes through a kind of microscope and may put drops in your eyes to *dilate,* or enlarge, your pupils. This helps the doctor see inside your eyes, and it doesn't hurt at all.

"I just got glasses. I was worried everybody would make fun of me, but I realized that after a while, no one will remember what I look like without them!"

Courtney

You're Not Alone

Your vision may continue to change during the time you're in grade school and level off when you reach your teens. If you're one of the first to get glasses, you may feel like the loneliest girl in the world. But peek around your classroom in a couple of years, and you'll find that you've got lots of company!

Glasses

Glasses are convenient and easy to care for. They come in lots of fun colors and styles. Some girls think of their eyeglasses as fashion accessories!

Contact Lenses

Contact lenses change the way you see without changing the way you look. But they're also expensive and require daily care and cleaning. Some girls don't feel ready for this responsibility.

Eye Protection

Your eyes can burn just like your skin. Wear sunglasses at the pool or beach or on the ski slope to protect your eyes from ultraviolet rays. Look for shades marked "UVA/UVB protection." Don't stare into the sun, and never look directly at an eclipse, even with sunglasses.

Mouth

A smile is an invitation that you wear on your face. It says "I'm a girl you want to know!" Make sure your smile is a warm greeting and a sign of good health by brushing up on the basics.

Fluoride Facts

Fluoride is a mineral that helps make teeth strong so they can resist cavities. If you live in a city, your water probably has some fluoride in it. Make sure your toothpaste does, too. And you don't need a huge gob of paste to get the job done—just a squirt about the size of a pea.

Toothbrush Basics

Choose a small-size toothbrush with soft, rounded bristles. Replace your brush every two to three months, or as soon as the bristles get droopy. Bent bristles won't clean your teeth properly, and they can harm your gums.

Daily Duty

Plaque is a gooey bacterial film that forms on your teeth. It can cause cavities and gum disease. Attack plaque! Brush your teeth first thing in the morning and at bedtime. Try to brush after eating, too. Pack a toothbrush in your backpack and slumber party kit so you won't be tempted to skip. Do it every day, the right way. No fair just swishing the toothpaste around a little! Correct brushing takes minutes, not seconds.

Tickle Your Tongue

Don't forget to brush your tongue, too! Freshly scrubbed taste buds are an important part of a clean mouth and fresh breath.

How to Brush

1 Hold your toothbrush at an angle to your gum line. Brush back and forth in small strokes, one tooth at a time. Repeat until you've scrubbed every single tooth.

2 Now do the inside of each tooth, using the same back-and-forth motion. Make sure to brush right up to the gum line.

3 Use the very tip of the brush to get behind your top and bottom front teeth.

1 Pull off a strand of floss about 18 inches long. Wind most of it around the middle finger of one hand, and the rest around the middle finger of the other.

2 Grip the floss between your thumbs and forefingers, stretching it tight. Push the floss gently between two of your teeth, wiggling it up and down the sides of both teeth and under the gum line. Imagine yourself scooping out little bits of food.

3 Unwind a little clean floss, winding up the used floss as you do so. Floss between two more teeth. Keep going, winding and flossing, until you've gone between all your teeth. Don't forget to floss at the very end of each row, behind your last tooth.

Healthy Gums

Think pink! Your gums need just as much attention as your teeth. If you don't take care of your gums, you could be setting yourself up for *gingivitis*—a disease that causes painful, red, swollen gums. To prevent gingivitis, floss once a day to fish out food lurking along the gum line. Dental floss comes in different thicknesses, waxed and unwaxed, to slide between your teeth comfortably. It even comes in tasty flavors!

Fresh Breath

Halitosis is a fancy way of saying "bad breath." But no matter what you call it, nothing shouts "Stand back!" quite as loudly. In rare cases mouth odor is caused by a nasal infection, upset stomach, or other problem that may need a doctor's attention. But it may just be a sign that you're skimping on brushing and flossing. Food between your teeth can rot and stink just like garbage. So clean it out!

Say "Cheese"!

Dairy products such as milk, cheese, and yogurt are good sources of *calcium,* a mineral that helps toughen up teeth. A balanced, healthy diet that limits gooey, chewy, sticky snacks is the smartest choice.

Regular Visits

Does going to the dentist make your teeth chatter? You'll be less afraid if you know what to expect. Before the exam, ask your dentist to explain what will happen. And remember, regular checkups are the best way to avoid cavities and other problems that require special treatment.

Braces

Braces are a short-term invest-
ment in your long-term smile!

Grin and Bare 'Em

Today, millions of Americans—girls, grown-ups, even movie stars—are proudly sporting tin grins. If you're about to get braces, you may be nervous about what others will think or say. Perhaps you're braced for taunts of "Hey, metal mouth!" or "Woo-woo, train tracks!" You can rain on a bully's parade by taking the lead yourself. Give one and all a super-dazzling smile. If you *show* that you're confident, it will help you *feel* confident.

"Remember, you're not the only one in the world who has braces. Even adults wear them. Just smile. Braces are cool!" *Briana*

A special brush called an *interproximal brush* scoots into the tight spots. Ask your ortho- dontist how to get one.

Brushing

Brushing your teeth carefully is more important now than ever because food can get trapped on brackets and under wires. You should brush after every meal or snack. And at least once a day, devote several minutes to scouring all the nooks and crannies. If you don't, you may be in for a shock when your braces come off—an ugly line of tooth decay right where the braces used to be!

Flossing

With braces, it's especially important to floss your teeth daily. Most dentists say that bedtime is a good time, since you're more likely to slow down and do it right. Ask your orthodontist to show you how to thread the floss above your brackets. There's even a nifty tool that you can use.

No-Go's

Hard foods can break your braces, and sticky foods will get, well, stuck in them. Cut apples and carrots into bite-size bits, and say "later" to caramels and gummy candy. For now, imagine the goodies you'll eat with your beautiful, straight teeth *after* the braces come off.

Rainbow Smile

Express your style every time you smile. You can choose rubber bands for your brackets in all sorts of colors, from pastels to Day-Glo brights. Ask your orthodontist what choices are available to you.

Face

The skin on your face doesn't need a bunch of fancy lotions or potions—just a little tender loving care.

A Gentle Wash

Wash your face thoroughly at least once a day, especially at bedtime. Use a mild soap or facial cleanser—not a deodorant soap or a body bar meant to be used in the bath or shower. Use your hands or a soft, clean washcloth to gently wash your face. Use warm, not hot, water and rinse your skin well to remove all traces of soap.

Hands Off!

One of the best things you can do for your face is to keep your hands off it! Your fingers can spread oil and bacteria. When you do need to touch your face, use clean hands. And never pick at pimples—you could turn a tiny flare-up into a big-time breakout that leaves a scar.

Chapped Lips

If your lips are chapped, soothe them with a swoosh of lip balm. Look for one with sunscreen in it. Also, make sure you're drinking enough water. Dry, cracked lips may be your body's way of croaking "Help—I'm thirsty!"

The Skin You're In

The skin on your face is thinner and more sensitive than on other parts of your body, so be choosy about what you put on it. Look for unscented soaps and lotions that are labeled *hypoallergenic,* which means free of ingredients that can be irritating. If your skin is oily or prone to pimples, choose facial products that are oil-free or *non-comedogenic*—not likely to clog your pores. If your skin is dry, dab moisturizer or lotion only on the spots where it's needed.

Almost every girl comes face-to-face with skin flare-ups at some time. But you don't need to lose your head over them.

Acne Attack

Zits! Blackheads! Whiteheads! All of these bumps and blemishes are part of the package known as *acne*. Acne can appear for several reasons. During puberty, your body produces more oil, which combines with bacteria and dead skin cells to clog your pores—and that causes pimples. Family history also makes some people more likely to get acne. If you feel like pimples are picking on you, you're not alone. Almost every girl and boy in your school will have a battle with skin blemishes at one time or another.

Striking Back

While occasional bouts of acne are practically unavoidable, you may be able to prevent a few blemishes from becoming a full-blown breakout.

Keep your face clean. Wash your face daily with a mild soap or cleanser, but don't overdo it. Harsh scrubbing and rubbing can irritate already bothered skin.

Don't pick at or pop pimples. The oils and dirt on your fingers will only fan the flames of a flare-up. Plus, you can cause a permanent scar on your skin.

Check out the drugstore. Acne products can provide some relief for mild breakouts. Cruise the skin-care aisle at the drugstore, and read the labels carefully. Products that contain *benzoyl peroxide* or *salicylic acid* help reduce oil and get rid of dead skin.

A product with benzoyl peroxide or salicylic acid may irritate sensitive skin. Before putting it on your face, test a little on the inside of your wrist to see if it gives you a rash. If it does, don't use it!

Talk to your doctor. Severe, out-of-control acne may call for medical attention. Your doctor can prescribe special creams or pills that are stronger than products available without a prescription.

Sun Sense

On bright, sunny days and on snowy days, too, always bring your "sun sense" along with you.

Here's an easy way to remember how to protect your skin from the sun:

Slip on clothing that covers your skin from the sun's rays.

Slap on a hat with a broad brim that shades your face, ears, and neck.

Slop on sunscreen before venturing outdoors.

No Safe Tans

You may think a tan looks great *now,* but wrinkles and spots don't look good on anyone. Doctors agree: there's no such thing as a safe tan. All skin, regardless of type, is damaged by the sun. Exposing your unprotected skin can give you a blistering-hot burn and lead to allergic reactions—and skin cancer.

Protect Your Skin

The sun's rays are most intense between ten o'clock in the morning and three o'clock in the afternoon, but dangerous rays are present all day long. Remember, too, that the sun can damage your skin even on cloudy days and in winter. The sun reflects off the clouds and snow, making it extra intense.

So before you head out the door, be sure to slather on some sunscreen. Sunscreen products carry a rating called an SPF, or sun protection factor. An SPF rating of 15 means that the sunscreen protects your skin 15 times longer than if you had used nothing at all. Everyone should use sunscreen with an SPF of at least 15. Girls with fair skin should use a product with an SPF of 30 or greater. Going swimming? Wear water-proof sunscreen with an SPF of at least 45, no matter what color skin you have.

Reapply Often

If you're spending a lot of time outside, bring your sunscreen along and slather on more every couple of hours. When you're at the beach or pool, it's especially important to reapply sunscreen after you get out of the water.

Beach Basics

Sandy beaches make the sun's rays even stronger. Take extra care by wearing lots of sunscreen and covering up with a hat and T-shirt. Of course, finding a shady spot to spend some time in is a good idea, too. Your skin will thank you!

Body Talk

Do you feel as if the whole world can spot every spot on your **face?** Keep your chin up. And give people something else to notice—your smile!

Freckle Face

I have freckles. I hate them and wish I could get some kind of lotion that would make my freckles go away. I need help!

FRECKLES

There's no magic potion or lotion that will make your freckles disappear. But wearing a hat and plenty of sunscreen when you go out in the sun may keep you from getting more spots. And the next time you look in the mirror, practice pairing your freckles with a grin. See? Smiles and freckles are a winning combo! The fact is, most of us have something we'd like to change about ourselves. But try to think of your freckles as a special feature, something extra that makes you uniquely YOU.

Cold Sores

I have a big, ugly sore on my face right next to my mouth. My mom says it's a cold sore, but I don't even have a cold! This isn't the first time I've had this problem, either. How do I get rid of it?

Sore Spot

Cold sores, also called *fever blisters,* don't have anything to do with the common cold. They're caused by a virus similar to the one that causes chicken pox. While cold sores aren't serious, they can be an occasional nuisance. They often flare up when you're sick or stressed out, although there's no way to predict exactly when you'll get one. There are products you can buy at the drugstore to help dry the sores up. If you have frequent, painful sores, your doctor may be able to prescribe stronger medication.

Bothersome Bangs

I just got bangs, but I've been having a problem with them. I've been getting pimples on my forehead. I've been washing my hair six times a week and putting medication on the pimples, but they still won't go away. Should I grow my bangs out?

Forehead Pimples

You are right to shampoo frequently. Girls who wear bangs need to keep their hair extra clean. Oils from your hair can irritate acne and make it worse. You'll also need to steer clear of hair products such as styling gels, sprays, and pomades that can leave a greasy film on your forehead. You don't have to banish bangs permanently, but you may need to pin them out of the way until your forehead clears up. Using headbands, barrettes, and other hair doodads is a fun and fashionable way to keep your bangs out of the zit zone. Ask the person who cuts your hair for some tips.

Zapped by Zits

I am ten years old and I have 13 zits. I've tried everything to get rid of them, but they always come back. I don't even eat a lot of junk food. Recently people have been calling me pizza face. What should I do?

Pizza Face

The sad truth is that you probably can't zap your zits completely. And though it's important to eat well, doctors agree that diet doesn't have much to do with acne. Talk to your doctor to see what else she recommends. Be patient. You may feel like you stand out now, but soon you won't be the only one under an acne attack. Pimples and puberty just seem to go together like pizza and pepperoni! The good news is that most acne clears up in the late teen years.

Reach!

Here's handy advice for grooming your **hands**

so you can wave a happy hello. Plus everything

you ever wanted to know about **underarms,**

from dealing with sweaty pits to smooth-shaving

tips. And, finally, answers to all your questions

about **breasts,** including hints for finding

bras that *really* fit.

Hands

Keep your hands well groomed so you can put your best fingers forward for meeting and greeting people.

Clean Hands Win!

Keeping your hands clean is your first line of defense against picking up germs and bacteria. Always wash your hands with soap and water after you use the restroom and before you eat. If you have a cold, wash up often—especially after you blow your nose!

Battling Bad Habits

If you bite your nails or suck your thumb or fingers, you're not alone. The good news is that lots of girls have been able to break their bad habits with one of these tried-and-true tricks:

- ❏ Hold on to a small object, such as a stone or a ball, to keep your hands busy and out of your mouth.
- ❏ Coat your nails with a special bad-tasting polish, available at the drugstore.
- ❏ Wear gloves or mittens to bed so you can't suck your thumb or fingers in your sleep.
- ❏ Set up a reward system. Use a calendar to keep track of how many days you go without giving in to your habit, and give yourself a treat if you meet your goal.

If all else fails, talk to a doctor or dentist for ideas. But don't give up—it takes time and patience to undo habits you've had for years.

Warts

Warts are harmless little bumps of flesh, usually white or pinkish in color. They're caused by viruses passed from one person to another. Warts often go away by themselves. You can also buy products at the drugstore to get rid of a wart, but they can take one to two months to work. If you don't want to wait, your doctor can remove a wart with a special freezing process.

Calluses

Calluses are hard, rough patches of skin caused by friction. Your body grows a layer of tough skin to protect the rubbed area. Athletes such as gymnasts get a lot of calluses, but you can get them just from raking leaves or gripping the handlebars of your bike. Wear gloves to help prevent calluses.

Nail Care

Scraggly, dirty fingernails are a sorry sight. Scrub your nails with a soft-bristled nail brush to remove the dirt trapped underneath.

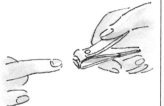

Once a week or so, use nail clippers to trim your nails. If you have a *hangnail,* a painful split in the skin alongside the nail, clip the hangnail down as closely as possible. Then leave it alone. Don't bite or pick at it. That will make it worse.

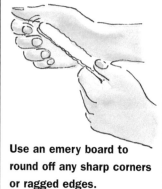

Use an emery board to round off any sharp corners or ragged edges.

Underarms

In the past you probably never gave your armpits a second thought. But now that you're growing up, it's time to start paying attention to them.

Antiperspirants help prevent pit stains. Your clothes—and your friends—will thank you!

B.O.—It's the Pits!

Sweating is natural and healthy. It's your body's way of cooling down. But you may be sweating more than ever before and in different places, such as under your arms. And when the sweat mixes with bacteria on your skin and meets the air, it can smell! Luckily, keeping body odor in check isn't hard. You can start by giving your armpits a good sudsing every time you shower or bathe.

Deodorants and Antiperspirants

Once you've washed your armpits, you may want to use an underarm product that helps keep the sweat, odor, or both away. *Deodorants* work to prevent underarm odor. *Antiperspirants* actually work to reduce sweating. Some products are both an antiperspirant and a deodorant. They come in roll-ons, solid sticks, gels, and sprays—pick the one that works best for you.

Underarm Hair

If you haven't already sprouted hair under your arms, you will soon. Some girls don't like it. Others aren't bothered by it one little bit. Whether you want to remove it or leave it there is a very personal decision. If you feel you'd be more comfortable without underarm hair, ask your mom if you can remove it. Shaving is the most common way to get rid of underarm hair. While shaving may seem scary at first, it quickly becomes second nature. Ask your mom or older sister for a lesson.

Shaving Tips

- ❏ Hair is softest when it's wet, so shave in the shower or bath. Whatever you do, *never* shave dry!
- ❏ Slick up your armpits with shaving cream or soap.
- ❏ Use short, downward strokes. You don't need to apply a lot of pressure.
- ❏ Rinse the razor frequently so it doesn't get clogged with hair.
- ❏ Replace your razor blade after two or three uses. A sharp blade is the secret to a smooth shave. Dull blades cause nicks.

Breasts

Budding breasts are one of the first signs that you're entering puberty and that your body is starting to take on a new shape.

Time to Grow

You'll probably start to notice changes in your breasts between the ages of 9 and 12, although some girls start earlier or later. There's no way to predict how big your breasts will get—you won't necessarily take after your mother or older sister. And don't worry if you notice one breast growing more quickly than the other. The two will eventually even out, although they'll never be exactly alike.

Stages of Development

Doctors divide breast development into the five stages shown below. See if you can tell what stage you're in, and sneak a peek at what's coming next.

If you don't seem to go through every stage, don't panic. Some girls may skip over one of the middle stages.

Stage 1
This is how most breasts look before puberty begins. Breasts are flat to the chest, with a raised nipple and small areola.

Stage 2
A raised bump called a *breast bud* begins to develop under each nipple. The nipples and areolas get larger and darker. You may feel some tenderness in this area as the breasts grow.

How Long Does It Take?

There's no way to know how long each stage will last or how long it will take for your breasts to become fully developed. Most girls reach stage 5 about four to five years after their breasts begin developing, or around age 17 or 18.

Shapes, Sizes, and Colors

Breasts come in endless varieties. Some are big, some are small. Some are round, some are more pointy. Some sit high on the chest, some hang low. Some point up, some point down. Even the colors of the nipples and *areolas,* the dark circular areas around the nipples, vary from pink to dark brown. Some nipples stick out, while others are *inverted,* or go inward. Some girls may discover small hairs growing around their areolas. This is normal. Don't pick at or try to pluck out the hairs. Doing so can irritate the sensitive skin in this area and cause an infection.

Stage 3

The nipple and areola continue to grow and get even darker in color. Breasts get larger and may look a bit pointy.

Stage 4

The areola and nipple blend together into a mound that rises above the breast. Some girls skip this stage.

Stage 5

Breasts are fully developed, with a rounder, fuller shape. The areola blends into the breast. The nipple is raised above it.

Do You Need a Bra?

There's no right answer to this question. There's only what's right for you. Do you feel self-conscious because your growing breasts show through your shirt? Are you uncomfortable when you play sports? Generally, you need a bra when you feel that you'd be more comfortable *with* one than *without* one.

"Girls should wear bras to be **comfortable.** It's up to the girl herself to decide when the time is right." *Katelyn*

First Things First

If you've decided it's time to get a bra, you'll need to talk with your mom or another adult family member before you head for the mall. Work up your courage and state your case as clearly as possible. Tell your mom or family member that you feel you're ready for a bra. Explain why you think you need one, and ask if she'll take you shopping for one. If she doesn't agree that you need one, offer to compromise by starting with a sports bra or training bra. They're described on pages 48–49.

No One Has to Know

What if you're ready to wear a bra but you're not ready for the whole world to know? Don't worry. Bras come in plenty of neutral colors that will match your skin tone. You don't have to buy the bras with bright colors or eye-popping prints that will show through your shirts.

Do you feel left out because everyone except you is getting a bra? Try a tank top or camisole under your shirt—no one will be able to tell if you're wearing a bra or not.

Sizing Up Sizes

Once you've decided to buy a bra, you'll need to figure out what size you wear. Bra sizes have two parts: a number and a letter. The number relates to the size of your rib cage. The letter—or cup size—relates to the size of your breasts. But don't worry too much about figuring out your exact bra size. It's only meant as a starting point. Every bra is different, and you may have to try on several different ones to find the right fit for you.

Adjusting the Fit

Once you've found the right size, you may still need to make some adjustments. Depending on the style of your bra, you may be able to tighten or loosen the fit around your rib cage by moving the hook over one or two notches. You may also be able to make the shoulder straps longer or shorter. To see if the straps are the right length, wiggle your shoulders. If the straps slide off, shorten them. If they feel as though they're biting into your skin, let them out a bit.

There's no reason to wear a bra while you sleep. It won't affect your shape or size. Put your bra on in the morning and take it off at night.

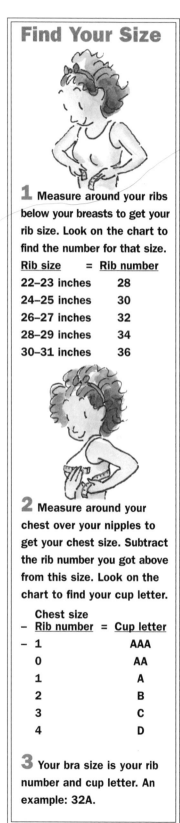

Find Your Size

1 Measure around your ribs below your breasts to get your rib size. Look on the chart to find the number for that size.

Rib size	=	Rib number
22–23 inches		28
24–25 inches		30
26–27 inches		32
28–29 inches		34
30–31 inches		36

2 Measure around your chest over your nipples to get your chest size. Subtract the rib number you got above from this size. Look on the chart to find your cup letter.

Chest size – Rib number	=	Cup letter
– 1		AAA
0		AA
1		A
2		B
3		C
4		D

3 Your bra size is your rib number and cup letter. An example: 32A.

Bra Browsing

Bras come in oodles of styles, fabrics, and colors. You'll need to try on lots to find a good fit, so look for a store with a large selection. Ask your mom, your older sister, or an adult friend to go with you. They can help adjust straps and fetch more sizes for you. When you find a bra that looks smooth under your shirt and doesn't pinch, scratch, or ride up your back, buy it!

Training Bras

A bra with an A to AAA cup is often called a *training bra*. This bra doesn't train your breasts to do anything—it trains *you* to get used to wearing a bra! Even if you don't need it for support, wearing one may make you feel less self-conscious and more confident about how you look.

Underwire Bras

Girls who wear a size C cup or larger may want the extra support of an *underwire bra.* This bra has a curved wire sewn into the fabric along the bottom of each cup. The extra stiffness helps hold the breasts in place, so they don't jiggle as much.

Soft-Cup Bras

You guessed it—*soft-cup bras* are soft and flexible. For most girls who wear a size B cup or smaller, the elastic band in a soft-cup bra provides all the support they need, plus a comfortable fit.

Sports Bras

A *sports bra* looks like a cut-off tank top with a wide elastic band at the bottom. It's designed to hold your breasts snugly against your chest so they don't bounce around while you're running or jumping. You can wear a sports bra every day if you like how it looks and feels.

Body Talk

Too big? Too small? No matter how they're built, many girls feel their **breasts** just aren't right. And that's just plain wrong!

Body Bullies

Some of the boys in my class make fun of me because my chest is practically flat! They are always making up poems and songs about me.

Tired of Boys

Rude remarks can really smart! What you need to do is remember to look at the big picture. Are your breasts really the most important part of you? No way! What about your straight A's in math, your perfect back flip, or your kindness to family and friends? That's the real you, the girl inside who really matters. Don't lose sight of her for a second, even when others seem to. If the teasing gets worse, or if a boy's words or actions make you feel threatened or afraid, tell a parent or teacher *immediately*. Nobody has the right to harass you or to make you feel unsafe.

Pump Up the Pasta?

I don't have any breasts! I was wondering if there were any foods to give me the nutrients to grow breasts.

flat Chest

Lots of girls wish there were a miracle diet or magic exercise that would make their breasts blossom overnight. But no food you eat will make a beeline to your breasts. And all the push-ups in the world won't increase your cup size. Breasts are made mostly of fatty tissue and milk ducts, so there are no muscles in them to flex. Beware of advertisements for diets, drugs, or fancy gadgets that claim to boost your bust. Their claims are just flat-out lies.

Faking It

I am really flat-chested. All the girls have big breasts except me. Should I stuff? I'm worried the tissue might fall out when I'm running.

Stuff?

Who wants wads of itchy tissue stuffed down her shirtfront? You don't need that sort of trickery. Chances are you won't fool anyone, but you might *feel* like a fool when some eagle eye calls your bluff. It's hard not to compare yourself to other girls or to the images you see on TV and in magazines, but never forget that it's the stuff in your head and heart—not the stuff in your sweater—that determines how you really measure up.

Too Busty

I have bigger boobs than all of my friends. Because of this, my friends are embarrassed to be around me because they think I'm very ugly and fat. I used to be very popular, but now I find myself dorky and lonely.

Desperate For Help

You're not dorky—you're *developing*. And though you wish otherwise, your body has a schedule all its own. For every girl like you who's sad because her breasts are growing quickly, there's another girl who's upset that hers are still flat. And it's just plain wrong for girls to be mean to someone because her body is changing. Choose outfits that make you feel comfortable and confident. Make sure your bra fits properly. You might even try wearing sports bras. Their extra-snug support may lift your spirits, too. No matter what you wear, stand up straight and proud. If you feel good about yourself, you'll be less of a target for teasers.

Belly Zone

This section is all about your midsection! Tall, short, straight, curvy—find out why all girls should celebrate their unique **shapes and sizes.** Learn how to **eat well** and be choosy about the **food** you chew. Get the straight facts about **eating disorders,** and learn what to do when food problems are eating at *you*.

Shapes & Sizes

All Different Shapes

The shape of your body—your basic frame—is something you're born with, like the shape of your nose or the color of your eyes. Some girls are tall and lanky, while others are short and sturdy. Some girls are curvy, while others are more straight. Usually your body shape resembles the shape of others in your family. No one body type is better or worse than another. All can be fit, healthy, and beautiful.

"Your weight depends on how your body is built. Also, your body hasn't finished **developing** yet. Just remember, you were made beautifully. Don't listen to anyone who says you're not!" *Sam*

Beware of "fad" diets and fancy weight-loss programs you see advertised in magazines. Always ask your doctor about a diet before you try it!

All Different Sizes

Many girls worry about whether their weight is "normal" for their age. But there's no such thing as one ideal weight, especially during puberty, when girls' bodies are growing quickly and changing shape. There's a wide range of weights that doctors consider normal for any girl, depending on her height and basic body type. If you're concerned about your weight, don't decide on your own to go on a diet. Talk to your doctor first to find out if it's necessary. Together you can set weight and fitness goals based on what's healthiest for you and what makes sense for your particular body type.

Where's My Waist?

As your body changes and your weight begins to shift, you may go through a period when your waist "thickens," or gets bigger. It doesn't mean you're getting fat. It means you're filling out. Your waistline will reappear as your body develops.

Food

Fuel up! Healthy eating habits give your body the extra energy it needs to grow during puberty.

Eating a Balanced Diet

There's really no such thing as "good food" or "bad food." It's true that some foods—such as whole grains and vegetables—have more nutrients than others. And some foods are higher in fat or sugar. But even chocolate cake and french fries have a place at the table if they are eaten only occasionally. The key is *moderation.* That means not eating too much or too little of anything. Make sure your meals and snacks are a mix of many different kinds of foods. No girl can live on candy bars or carrot sticks alone.

Knowing When to Eat

Do you eat when you're bored? Do treats and TV go together? Do you reach into the fridge out of habit, whether you're hungry or not? You may be eating when you don't need to. How do you know when to eat? Listen to your body. Try to eat only when you're hungry, and stop when you're full. Eat a snack if you think you need an energy boost. But don't eat just because you're nervous, bored, or craving a favorite flavor. Eating should be a pleasure, not a pastime.

Smart Snacks

For most girls, three square meals aren't enough to get through a busy day. Mini meals of fruit, raw veggies, cheese, low-fat yogurt, or whole-grain crackers spread with nut butter can fill in the gaps. When you're packing your lunch, include a healthful snack to munch on between school and soccer or ballet and babysitting.

Best Beverages

Water is hands down the best beverage around, and your body thirsts for it. Make sure you drink plenty of it every day, especially during and after exercise. Soda pop and punch—even fruit juices—are high in sugar and should be viewed as "seldom snacks." Low-fat milk is always a healthier choice.

Going Vegetarian

Thousands of girls and their families have chosen to eliminate meat and other animal products from their diets. Some do it because of their beliefs. Others do it for health reasons. A vegetarian diet can easily supply all the nutrients you need. But if you're thinking about becoming a vegetarian, first do some homework. It isn't simply a matter of passing over the hamburger and filling up on fries. You'll need to learn what foods to eat to get enough protein, vitamins, and minerals.

Be sure to pack your meals and snacks with foods from the major food groups every day.

A Balancing Act

Just how much from each food group should you eat every day? That depends on your age and how physically active you are. The United States Department of Agriculture (USDA) says that a girl who is ten years old and gets 30 to 60 minutes of moderate to vigorous exercise a day should aim to eat the following:

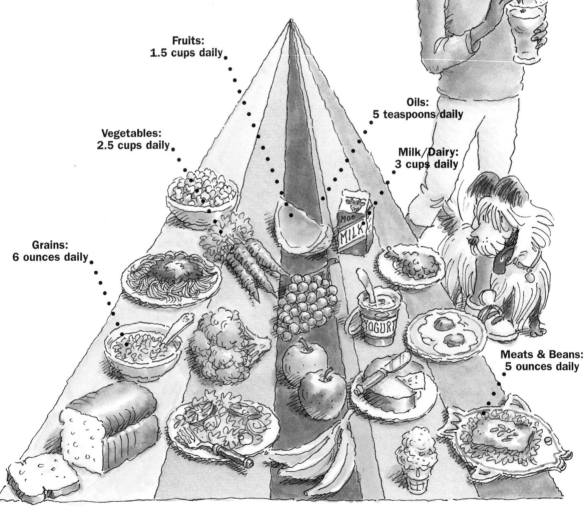

Fruits:
1.5 cups daily

Oils:
5 teaspoons daily

Vegetables:
2.5 cups daily

Milk/Dairy:
3 cups daily

Grains:
6 ounces daily

Meats & Beans:
5 ounces daily

What Counts as an Ounce or Cup?

Good question! Here's an example from each of the food groups:

Grains: One slice of bread equals 1 ounce.

Vegetables: One scoop of cooked veggies about the size of a tennis ball equals 1 cup.

Fruits: An apple about the size of your fist equals 1 cup.

Oils: A handful of nuts equals about 5 teaspoons.

Milk/Dairy: One piece of cheese as big as a Ping-Pong ball equals 1 cup.

Meats & Beans: One piece of meat about the size of a deck of cards equals about 2.5 ounces.

Be a Savvy Snacker

Instead of . . .

french fries

a bowl of ice cream

a bag of chips

a milk shake

Grab . . .

popcorn sprinkled with Parmesan cheese

low-fat frozen yogurt

a handful of roasted almonds

a fresh-fruit smoothie

Tips

☐ Make sure half of your grains are whole grains.
☐ Eat a rainbow of colorful veggies, from green kale to orange squash!
☐ Choose whole fruits whenever possible instead of drinking fruit juices.
☐ Rely on low-fat or fat-free milk, yogurt, cheese, and other dairy products.
☐ Go easy on processed meats such as hot dogs, pepperoni, and sausage.
☐ Heap your plate with foods made from dried beans, split peas, and other legumes. Not only are they nutritional powerhouses; they also count as either a vegetable or a meat/bean choice!

Less Is Best

Beyond the basic food groups, you are also allowed "discretionary calories," a fancy name for extras such as the oils, fats, sugars, and salt that are in many of the foods you eat. These should be eaten sparingly. A little butter or sweetener goes a long way.

Your Personal Food Pyramid

Every girl's dietary needs are different. To find out what the USDA says is a balanced diet for you, ask a parent, teacher, or librarian to help you look online at www.mypyramid.gov.

What makes a girl glow from head to toe? A daily diet rich in all the essential vitamins and minerals!

Vitamin A

For sparkling eyes, sharp night vision, and smooth skin: eat apricots, nectarines, carrots, spinach, sweet potatoes, and squash.

Vitamin B

For healthy red blood cells and plenty of energy: eat meat, fish, poultry, whole-grain products, leafy green vegetables, and dried beans.

Vitamin C

For strong teeth, gums, bones, and muscles and to ward off colds: eat oranges, strawberries, broccoli, peppers, spinach, and cabbage.

Vitamin D

For strong teeth and bones: drink lots of milk and eat eggs, salmon, and liver.

Vitamin E

To protect the tissue in your skin, eyes, liver, and lungs: eat sunflower seeds, leafy green vegetables, nuts, avocados, and foods made with corn oil.

Vitamin K

For blood that clots quickly when you're cut: eat broccoli, spinach, lettuce, cabbage, and cheese.

Iron

For a healthy blood supply that's full of oxygen: eat red meat, baked potatoes, apricots, raisins, dried beans, and whole-grain breads.

Calcium

For straight, tall posture and a great grin: eat yogurt, cheese, and broccoli. Drink three to four glasses of milk a day.

Eating Disorders

Eating disorders are serious illnesses that can destroy a girl's health and well-being and even threaten her life.

Out of Control

Lots of people worry about their weight and wish they could be thinner, but when a girl becomes so focused on losing weight that she stops eating normally, she may have an eating disorder. Living with this kind of illness can be very hard. A girl's fierce desire to be thin can quickly spiral into dangerous habits and behaviors that she can't control. No matter how thin she becomes, she looks in the mirror and sees a fat girl. Without help, she can become very sick. She can do permanent damage to her body, or even die. There are two main eating disorders: *anorexia* (an-uh-REX-ee-uh) and *bulimia* (buh-LEE-mee-uh).

Anorexia

Anorexia nervosa is an eating disorder that causes a girl to starve herself. To control her weight, she becomes obsessed with ways to avoid food. She may even develop special rituals for how to eat, in order to eat as little as possible. As she gets thinner and thinner, she begins to have serious medical problems. She can even lose so much weight that she literally starves to death. An anorexic girl may:

❑ refuse to eat, or eat only small amounts.
❑ eat only "safe" foods—foods low in calories and fat.
❑ play with her food or cut it up to make it look eaten.
❑ exercise constantly.
❑ wear baggy clothes because she's convinced she doesn't look good in anything else.

Bulimia

A girl who suffers from *bulimia* is also obsessed with being thin. But unlike an anorexic, she doesn't starve herself to control her weight. Instead, she "binges" and then "purges." That means she eats a large amount of food in a short period of time and then tries to get rid of it by forcing herself to vomit, or by using laxatives that cause her to go to the bathroom. A girl who is bulimic may:

❏ become very secretive about food—about what, when, and how much she eats.

❏ save up or hide food.

❏ spend a lot of time thinking about and planning her next eating binge.

❏ take a lot of diet pills and laxatives.

❏ have stomach aches, sore throats, or tooth decay from frequent vomiting.

Getting Help

If you are struggling with an eating disorder, get help *now.* Don't let embarrassment force you to hide your problem. You have an illness that's not your fault. Talk to your parents or another adult you trust so you can get the treatment you need. Don't suffer alone—this problem is too big for any girl to tackle by herself.

"When I was 11, I stopped eating. I had to be hospitalized, and it took **counseling** for me to get back to normal. I now know that as you get older, you need to gain weight."

no name please

Body Talk

Weight worries and **food** fears can make some girls miserable at mealtime.

Fat or Thin?

People say I'm thin, but I think I need to lose about 15 pounds. I'm 11 years old and weigh a whopping 90 pounds. Don't I need to lose some weight?

Too Fat

Ask your doctor. If she says your weight is fine, then it is! But your thinking may need some shaping up. When some girls see super-skinny people in ads and on TV, they get tricked into worrying about their own bodies. They see themselves as fat when they're not. This can be unhealthy if it causes a girl to try to lose weight when she shouldn't. If you don't believe people when they say you're slim, talk with your doctor or your school counselor. They can help you see yourself just as you are—and teach you to like what you see.

Fear of Anorexia

I want to stay in good shape and look great, but with all the stuff I hear about eating disorders, I'm scared. I'm afraid I might become anorexic. I know once you've got it, it can be very obsessive and it can control your life. How do I stay away from it without overeating?

FREAKED!

Anorexia is a disorder in which a girl is so overly afraid of being fat that she starves herself. She is unable to see her body in a realistic way. To avoid anorexia and to keep your body fit and healthy, keep your *attitude* healthy. Instead of focusing on the amount you eat, focus on choosing nutritious, good-tasting foods and let yourself enjoy eating them! Get regular exercise in activities you find fun. Above all, remember that no one needs a perfect body to have a wonderful life.

Junk-Food Junkie

I have a problem with eating junk food. I am thin now, but soon all this eating will catch up to me and my weight. Plus, junk food is not good for your complexion. How can I get off my urge to eat and eat and EAT junk food?

WORRIED

Eating junk food every now and then is not necessarily a health disaster. And doctors no longer believe that it causes skin woes. The problem with junk food is that it simply doesn't have much nutritional value—it fills you up without giving you the nutrients you need. There's no quick fix to nix your junk-food cravings. Try cutting back gradually by substituting healthier snacks, such as fruit instead of cookies, or frozen yogurt instead of ice cream. Don't expect to cut junk food out of your life entirely. It's easier to allow yourself an occasional treat than to stick to a strict, junk-food-free diet.

Bulimia

I have a friend who has a big problem. She thinks she is fat but she really isn't. Everything she eats, she makes herself throw up. My friends and I are really worried. We tell her to stop, but she says she can't. I'm afraid she is going to hurt herself. What should we do?

Afraid

You are right to be frightened for your friend. She may be suffering from bulimia, a serious eating disorder. What you must do is tell an adult *immediately*. Talk to your parents, a teacher, a school counselor, or another adult you trust. Your friend needs professional help. She needs your love and support, too. But be prepared. Instead of thanking you for your concern, your friend may be upset, even angry. She may feel that you have betrayed her by revealing her secret. Be patient and stand by your friend in this stormy time. You're doing the right thing. And one day, when she's well again, your friend will realize that you took action because you cared about her.

Big Changes

Whether you've already sprouted hair in your **pubic area** and started your **period,** or whether you're still waiting for these big changes to happen, this section answers all the important questions, from tips on **tampons** and **pads** to the truth about **PMS.** Armed with the facts, you'll be able to *relax*.

Pubic Area

The area below your belly button will undergo some pretty big changes during puberty.

It's normal for pubic hair to appear over a period of years, so don't be surprised if this process seems as slow as watching grass grow.

Pubic Hair

The appearance of hair in your *pubic area* and on your *vulva* is one of the first signs that puberty is beginning. Your pubic area is the V-shaped patch of skin between your hip bones and your legs. The folds of skin and tissue between your legs are the vulva. Before puberty begins, you may have no hair in these areas at all. Or you may have a few soft, wispy hairs. At the start of puberty, these hairs begin to grow and darken. They may or may not match the color of the hair on your head. Eventually they grow in more thickly, becoming coarse and curly and forming a triangular patch. As you get older, your pubic hair may spread down onto the tops of your inner thighs. Some women also get a trail of hair leading up to their navel.

Other Changes

You may notice a sticky discharge in your underpants. This discharge is coming from your *vagina.* (See pages 70 and 76–77 to learn more about the vagina.) The discharge is usually clear or whitish and has very little smell. If it looks greenish or has a strong odor, or if your vulva feels itchy or swollen, see your doctor. You may have an infection.

To help prevent infections, keep the area between your legs clean and dry. It's important to wash regularly to get rid of all the sweat and bacteria that gather there. Avoid bubble baths, heavily scented soaps, and scented toilet paper. The perfumes can irritate the vagina and the delicate skin of your vulva.

Strip Clean

Take off damp or sweaty clothes as soon as possible. Bathing suits, tights, and leotards made of nylon and other synthetic fabrics can cause rashes and infections. Be sure to wash these garments frequently.

Get into Cotton

Whether you wear bikinis or briefs, buy underpants that are made of all cotton or have a cotton lining. Cotton *breathes,* or lets moisture pass through and evaporate. That means less risk of irritation and infection.

Fresh Start

Put on a clean pair of underpants at the start of every day and after every shower or bath. It's the simplest way to stay fresh.

Period

Getting your period. There are probably no other words that will make you feel as excited, scared, or just plain confused.

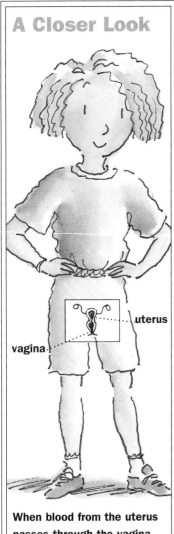

A Closer Look

uterus

vagina

When blood from the uterus passes through the vagina, you get a *menstrual period.*

The Basic Facts

So what's a period, anyway? It's short for *menstrual period*—the period of time each month when fluid containing blood flows out of the *uterus* through the *vagina*. The amount is small, only 4 to 6 tablespoons. This flow usually lasts two to eight days. Some girls have a menstrual period every 25 days. Other girls get them up to 40 days apart. All are normal. When you first start getting your period, though, the length of time between each period—and number of days the blood flow lasts—may change from one month to the next. After a while your periods will get more regular.

At first, the idea of getting periods may seem, well—*gross*. But periods are a sign that your body is healthy and working properly. It's preparing to do the grown-up work of having a baby someday. Every month your body practices for this by building a "nest," a place for a baby to grow inside your uterus. The nest is a lining of blood and other fluid that builds up on the uterus walls. Because there's no baby, the lining is shed and you have a period. It's all controlled by hormones, the chemicals that change your body from little girl to grown-up woman.

Telltale Signs

Most girls start to get periods between the ages of 9 and 15. You can't predict exactly when you'll get your first period, but your body may give you clues that it's on its way. Most girls start to *menstruate,* or get periods, about one to two years after their breasts have started developing and their pubic hair has begun growing in. Can other people tell whether you've gotten your period yet? Nope! Not unless you tell them.

Your First Time

So the day comes when you get your period. It may announce itself with a bright red, rusty red, or dark brown stain in your underpants. What do you *do*? Don't panic. Wipe yourself as well as you can. If you haven't got a pad or tampon—or you don't know how to use one—fold up a wad of toilet paper, Kleenex, or paper towel to put into your underwear.

Find your mom, an older sister, or a woman you trust. Take a deep breath and say, "I think I just got my period. Do you have something I can use?" You may feel like crawling into a hole, but remember, getting your period is *normal.* There's no reason to be ashamed. The older person will probably remember how it felt *her* first time and will be glad to help.

Keep a supply of pads or tampons on hand so you're always prepared. Once you know you won't be taken by surprise, you can R-E-L-A-X.

If your period catches you by surprise at school, ask a teacher or school nurse for help.

Buying Supplies

Deciding which "feminine hygiene" products to use can seem overwhelming at first, but your choices are actually pretty simple: *pads* or *tampons.* Pads fit into the crotch of your underpants and are made of layers of absorbent material that collect blood as it leaves your body. Tampons are inserted into the vagina and absorb the blood before it leaves your body. Both come in a variety of shapes, sizes, and absorbencies. You'll probably need to experiment to find what works best for you, depending on the activities you do and whether your blood flow is light or heavy. You may

Pads

Pads are convenient and easy to use. Some pads have a sticky strip on the back that attaches to your underpants. Others have wide "wings" that wrap around the edges of your underpants for added coverage.

Panty Liners

Panty liners, or panty shields, are very thin pads. They're best for days when your flow is light, or when you suspect your period might start and you want to be prepared. Some girls like to wear a panty liner along with a tampon in case the tampon leaks.

want to keep different products on hand for different days of the month and types of activities.

Scented vs. Unscented

Most pads and tampons are available in both deodorant and nondeodorant versions. Deodorant products have perfumes and other chemicals to fight odor caused by fluids and moisture trapped in the pad or tampon. But they can also irritate skin and cause allergic reactions. You're better off using unscented products and keeping yourself fresh by changing your pads and tampons regularly.

Tampons

Tampons are good for sports, especially swimming, because they're worn inside the body. The vagina muscles hold the tampon in place so it can't slip out. A string hangs outside your body so you can pull the tampon out. For more information about using a tampon, see pages 76–77.

When to Change

It's a good idea to replace your pad or tampon every two to four hours to prevent leaks and odor. If you have to go to the bathroom in the meantime, you can hold the string of the tampon out of the way so it doesn't get wet. Never leave a tampon in place for more than eight hours—you could get a serious infection called *toxic shock syndrome.* At night, use a pad. Change pads right before you go to bed and again first thing in the morning.

What to Do with the Used One

Whether you're at home or away, be sure to dispose of your used pads, tampons, applicators, and outer wrappings appropriately. This means wrapping pads in toilet paper and placing them in the nearest wastebasket. Some public rest rooms have a bin in each stall for this purpose. *Never* flush a pad down the toilet. Tampons can usually be flushed, but not all applicators. Check to see if the box says "flushable applicators." If not, wrap the applicator in toilet paper and throw it out.

Is It Over Yet?

Once your periods become regular, which usually happens within one to two years, they should last about the same length of time each month. You'll be able to tell when your period is winding down because the flow is usually heaviest in the beginning or middle and then starts to trickle off toward the end. You may not see any blood on the pad or in the tampon for several hours or even a whole day. The color may change, too—from bright red to brown. It's a good idea to wear a panty liner for a day or two even after you *think* your period is over. If you go more than two days without seeing any blood, your period is probably finished.

Wrappers from tampons and pads go in the wastebasket— not down the toilet.

Keeping Track

At first, it can be tricky to predict when your periods will arrive. Use a calendar to keep track of when they start and end. After a while, your cycle should become regular enough for you to be able to figure out when to expect your period.

A Closer Look

applicator
tampon

To get the hang of using a tampon, practice pushing it through its applicator.

tampon
uterus
vagina

When you insert a tampon, put it in at an angle to follow the slant of your vagina. There's no way the tampon can go into your uterus or anywhere else—there aren't any openings that the tampon could get through.

How to Insert a Tampon

For most girls, using a tampon is a little scary at first because it involves a part of the body that may be unfamiliar to you. But don't worry. With patience and practice, you'll be a pro in no time. Be sure to carefully read the instructions that come in the box of tampons, and remember the simple steps below.

uterus
vagina
tampon
applicator
urethra
vagina opening

1 Get Ready

Wash your hands. Remove the outer wrapper of the tampon. Hold the applicator tube with your thumb, middle finger, and forefinger, as shown. With the other hand, find the opening of your vagina. It's just below your *urethra*, where urine comes out. Use your fingers to spread apart the vagina opening.

2 Insert

Insert the tip of the applicator, aiming at a slight angle toward your back. Relax your muscles. Guide the applicator into your vagina. Then push on the inner tube of the applicator with your forefinger. This will push the tampon all the way up into your vagina. Pull out the applicator and throw it away.

Try starting out with "junior," "slim," or "slender" tampons. They're made for beginners and girls with small bodies.

Some tampons don't come with an applicator. They're inserted with your finger. You may want to wait till you're more comfortable with tampons before you use this kind. If you do use them, be sure to wash your hands *thoroughly* before and after inserting them.

Don't use a tampon with a torn wrapper. It may not be clean, especially if it's been bouncing around in your backpack for a while.

3 Check Fit

The string should now hang down between your thighs. If the tampon is in correctly, you won't be able to feel it. If it feels uncomfortable, it may be in crooked or may not be in far enough. Use your finger to push it up farther, or pull it out and start over with a new tampon. Wash your hands afterward.

4 Removal

When it's time to take out the tampon, relax your muscles and pull down on the string. The tampon will slide out of your vagina. It's not a good idea to flush the tampon down the toilet. Instead, wrap it in toilet paper and throw it out. Wash your hands when you're through.

What Is PMS?

Once you begin to menstruate regularly, you may notice some patterns in how you feel right before your period. Sometimes these physical and emotional changes are referred to as *premenstrual syndrome,* or PMS for short. It's not a disease or an illness, just a natural part of your menstrual cycle. PMS is caused by hormones—chemicals that are released in your body at this time. The symptoms you feel can be a clue to when your period is coming, so you'll want to pay attention to them.

Physical Signs

Up to two weeks before your period, your breasts may feel swollen or more tender than usual. You may also notice that your body feels heavier, even puffy, and that your skin is more prone to breakouts. All of these symptoms will go away after your period begins. You may also feel cramps in your lower abdomen or back before and during your period. The cramps are because the muscles of the uterus are hard at work.

Emotional Signs

Your periods can also affect your moods. Some girls feel tired, irritated, grouchy—more emotional—in the days leading up to their periods. If you find that your feelings are more intense during this time, know that this is perfectly normal. But when you're feeling extra edgy, try not to unleash your frustration on family and friends. Instead, try talking to them about how you feel. Doing so may bring kind words of support just when you need them most. And don't forget to treat yourself to some quiet time alone. Listen to music, take a walk, or write in a journal. You'll be glad you did!

Your feelings are important, so pay attention to them. Don't let anyone tell you they're stupid or silly, or that they don't matter.

How to Feel Better

The best remedies for premenstrual aches and pains are fairly simple: eat right, exercise, and treat yourself to some soothing heat.

Ahhh—Heat!

A warm bath or a hot-water bottle laid over your tummy can help soothe cramps.

Medications

If headaches, backaches, or cramps make you feel crummy, there is medication at the drugstore that you can try. Talk to your mom or doctor to see what she recommends.

Healthy Eating

Cut down on salty foods such as pretzels and chips before your period. Salt makes your body retain water, giving you that puffy, bloated feeling. Eat plenty of fruits and veggies instead.

Exercise

Stay active! Exercise is a great way to ease aches and pains and to lift your spirits, too. A brisk walk, a few laps in the pool, or a bike ride in the fresh air is always good medicine.

Body Talk

If you feel like your menstrual cycle is taking you for a ride, don't worry. In no time at all, you'll learn to take your **periods** in stride.

Sneak Attacks

What if my period starts in school or in church or in a public place and I don't have a pad or tampon? And what if it leaks on my clothes before I can stop it?

Scared

If you get caught unprepared, don't panic. Make a temporary pad out of folded toilet paper, Kleenex, or paper towel to put in your underpants. Then ask the school nurse, a teacher, or a friend if she has a spare pad or tampon. Some public restrooms have coin-operated machines where you can buy pads and tampons. If you do leak, tie a sweater, shirt, or jacket around your waist to make a fashionable cover-up until you can change clothes. Chances are, nobody will notice a thing! P.S. Cold water is best for getting blood stains out of clothes.

Tampons vs. Pads

How are you supposed to know if a tampon is better for you than a pad?

Just wondering

It all depends on what you're most comfortable with. Both are safe and reliable if used properly, so you really can't go wrong either way. Some girls who play sports prefer tampons because they don't show through a uniform or bathing suit, and they can be worn in water. Some girls like tampons because they keep you feeling dry— you can hardly tell you have your period! But other girls like pads because they're just plain simple to use. They're easy to change, and easy to know *when* to change. Don't be afraid to experiment with tampons and pads to figure out which you like best.

Miserable, Period.

I've had my period for a year now, and I still haven't gotten used to walking around feeling like I've wet my pants. I'm the only one of my girlfriends who has it. My mom is here to talk to me about it, but I don't want to. I don't want to keep it to myself, either. I feel like I don't even want to grow up!

I don't want to grow up!

You sound lonely, scared, *and* uncomfortable, and that's too heavy a load for any girl to bear. For starters, it might help to change your pad more often or consider giving tampons a try. Both will make you feel drier. Next, you need to screw up your courage—every ounce you can muster— and talk to an adult you trust. If you can't face your mom, pick an aunt, a teacher, a doctor, or a school counselor. It may be hard to imagine now, but talking it out with an adult who has "been there, done that" will make you feel much better.

Left Out

Everybody in my class has become a "woman" and I am still just a "girl." When everyone talks about being "women," I just hang back.

Maxi Pad

It's heartbreaking to feel that your friends are leaving you behind just because their bodies are changing at a different pace than yours. But that doesn't make these girls "women." There's a lot more to being an adult than getting your period and growing breasts. Still, your classmates may be feeling excited about the changes they're going through, maybe even a little afraid. And that's why they need to talk about them so much. Instead of feeling left out, can you listen in? Ask your friends questions about their experiences. You may get firsthand information that will help you when *your* day comes.

On the Go

Get a leg up on grooming your growing **legs** and protecting your **feet** from pain and odor. Learn how to turn **fitness** into fun, and to practice **sports safety** with the right equipment, exercises, and first-aid basics. And when it's time to **rest,** here's advice on how to get a good night's **sleep** so you can start every day fresh and ready to get into gear!

Give your legs a hand for all that hard work they do to keep you up and running!

If you think you're ready to start shaving your legs, talk it over with a parent first.

Growing Pains

During puberty, you're going to shoot up in height. Your legs in particular are going to lengthen and grow. For a period of time you may feel like your body is all legs. This rapid growth may also cause a tired, achy, cramped feeling in your legs. These occasional *growing pains* usually go away after puberty. And don't worry if your legs seem out of proportion for a while—the rest of you will soon catch up!

And Growing Hair

About the time you start to grow hair under your arms, you may notice that you're sprouting more hair on your legs, too. This hair is usually darker and coarser below the knee than above it. Though there's no real reason to remove leg hair, many girls prefer the look and feel of smooth shins. But once you begin removing leg hair, it may feel coarse and "stubbly" for a time as it grows back, and it may be more noticeable during this phase. So if you start shaving, you'll want to make it a regular part of your grooming routine from now on.

Shave Where?

Most girls shave only the hair on their shins and calves, south of the knees. The hair above the knees is usually so fine that it's not necessary to remove it—and it's an awful lot of leg to shave!

How to Shave

1 You'll need to buy a razor with replaceable blades or a supply of disposable razors. Disposable razors are easy to use but good for only a few shaves. A razor with replaceable blades is less wasteful, but changing the blades can be tricky.

2 Get your legs good and wet. You're more likely to nick yourself if your skin and hair aren't thoroughly moistened. Lather on a generous amount of soap or shaving cream or gel.

3 Start at the bottom and pull the razor slowly and gently up your leg with long, smooth strokes. Be careful around your ankles and knees, where it's easy to nick yourself. If you do cut yourself, rinse the cut with cold water, dry it off, and put a Band-Aid on it.

4 Stop to rinse your razor often so it doesn't get clogged with hair. When you're done shaving, rinse the razor before storing it away. Out of courtesy to other family members, rinse out the shower or tub, too.

5 After drying off, apply some lotion to your legs to soothe and moisturize the skin.

Your feet take a lot of pounding! Don't let foot and toe woes leave you standing on the sidelines.

P.U.! Foot Odor

The best way to deal with foot odor is to prevent it. Don't go sockless! Wear clean cotton socks that absorb sweat, with shoes made of natural materials such as leather or canvas that let feet breathe. Plastic and other synthetic materials are a recipe for smelly, sweaty feet. To de-stink your shoes, sprinkle baking soda in them and let them sit overnight. Shake out the baking soda—and the smell—in the morning.

Ouch! Blisters

Blisters are sore spots that develop where your shoes rub against your skin. The friction causes the skin to form a bubble, which sometimes pops or tears open. *Don't* pop the blister yourself. Place a Band-Aid over it to protect it until the skin can heal. You may want to remove the Band-Aid at night to expose the blister to air. This helps speed the healing.

On Your Toes

To keep your toes in tip-top condition, give them a little extra attention.

When you shower or bathe, be sure to scrub between your toes. Use a nailbrush to scour under the nails.

Trim your toenails regularly after showering or bathing, when the nail is softest and easiest to cut. Use nail clippers to cut straight across. This helps prevent *ingrown toenails,* which occur when a sharp corner of the nail grows into the skin.

Give your toes room to wiggle! Never buy shoes that don't fit, no matter how much you like them—you'll be in too much pain to enjoy how you look. Always measure your feet before buying new shoes.

Itchy! Fungus

You don't have to be an athlete to get *athlete's foot,* a fungus that spreads in damp places where people go barefoot, such as locker rooms and pools. You can prevent it by wearing flip-flops or shower shoes. If you notice itching and peeling on the bottoms of your feet, especially around the toes, you may have a case. Luckily, it's easy to treat with powders and sprays available at the drugstore.

Fitness

Whether it's skating or swimming, kickball or karate, find a fun way to stay fit. Pretty soon you'll forget it's good for you!

Active Girl = Healthy Girl

You already know that eating a balanced diet is essential to good health. But many girls forget that regular exercise is just as important. In addition to helping you look and feel shipshape, exercise strengthens your heart, gives you energy, helps you sleep better, makes your muscles stronger and more flexible, and builds self-confidence. So get up, get out, and get into gear!

How Much Is Enough?

Doctors and fitness experts recommend at least one hour of physical activity every day, including 30 minutes of *aerobic exercise* at least three times a week. Aerobic exercise is any activity that raises your heart rate and speeds up your breathing. How do you know if your body is working hard enough? Here's a good rule of thumb: when you're exercising or playing, if you're breathing too hard to sing but you can talk fairly easily, you're going at a good pace.

Just remember that whatever type of exercise you choose, don't get too hung up on counting minutes or monitoring your heart rate. The most important thing is to find fun activities that you love and to do them often.

You don't have to be a super-jock to stay in shape. Are you lousy at basketball and softball? Give bowling or strolling a try!

It Adds Up

Do you take the escalator when you could climb the stairs? Do you bug your mom for a ride when you're only going a few blocks? A few simple changes to your daily routine can make a difference.

❑ Ride your bike to the library instead of taking the bus.

❑ Volunteer for muscle-building chores, such as weeding the garden or raking leaves.

❑ Play a game of tag with your little sister or brother.

❑ Take the dog for a long walk.

Sports Safety

Even the best athletes can get injured if they're not careful. Play it smart! These simple strategies will help you stay in the game.

S-T-R-E-T-C-H

Follow these stretching secrets to help prevent injuries and to build strength and flexibility.

❏ *Stretch slowly.* No matter how excited you are to get into the game or back to the locker room, don't rush. The whole point is to ease your muscles *carefully* into or out of your workout, and that takes time.

❏ *Don't bounce.* Bobbing up and down can damage your muscles. Once you strike your stretching position, hold the pose. But don't forget to breathe!

❏ *Hold it!* Try to hold your stretch for a count of at least ten to be sure your muscles get the message.

❏ *Stretch both sides.* When limbering up your arms, legs, waist, or neck, be sure to give equal time to the front, back, left, and right sides.

Warm Up, Cool Down

Whether you're hiking, biking, or spiking a volleyball, always take time to stretch out your muscles and prepare them for the work they're about to do. A proper warm-up eases your body into gear and helps prevent muscle pulls and tears. At the end of your workout, cool down with more gentle stretching. This reduces stiffness and soreness the next day.

Wear the Right Gear

You probably already know how important it is to wear your helmet when biking or inline skating. But it might not occur to you to wear bright clothes so cars can see you coming! And don't head out on skates without elbow, wrist, and knee guards. Other sports may call for a mouth guard or special padding—check with your coach to see what's recommended. Always wear shoes and clothing that fit properly. High-tops that don't fit snugly can lead to twisted ankles. Skates that are too small are an invitation for blisters.

Don't Overdo It

Pay attention to how your body feels while you're exercising or playing a sport. If you're in pain, are getting dizzy or sick to your stomach, or are unable to catch your breath, stop immediately and rest. All of these are warning signs to slo-o-o-w down.

Drink LOTS of Water

When you're active, your body keeps you cool by producing sweat. You need to replace the fluids your body is losing by drinking lots of water before, during, and after you exercise. Fill up a sports bottle before you get going, and refill it often.

To be healthy, your body needs plenty of rest. Sleep is your body's way of recharging to meet the challenges of each new day.

Good Night!

What's the secret to a sound night's sleep? Develop sound sleeping habits. Getting enough rest helps you look and feel your very best.

Stick to a regular bedtime. One of the best ways to ensure a good night's sleep is to get up and go to bed at the same time every day. If you sleep late one morning, then get up early the next, you may feel tired and groggy all day and have trouble sleeping that night.

Develop a routine. It's a good idea to create a ritual, a special routine, that tells your body it's time to go to sleep. Listen to gentle music, take a warm bath, read a book, or write in a journal. Try to repeat your ritual every night at the same time.

Exercise. Active girls who exercise regularly are often the soundest sleepers of all. Exercise helps release extra energy and tension that can interfere with sleep. But don't exercise too close to bedtime or you may have trouble winding down!

Watch what you drink. Many sodas—especially colas—contain a substance called *caffeine* that can make you feel jumpy and wide awake. Caffeine is also in coffee, tea, and chocolate. Avoid anything with caffeine at night, especially close to bedtime.

Don't go to bed stuffed. A tummy that's churning because it's too full makes a bad bunk-mate. If your stomach is growling from hunger, though, a glass of milk before bedtime is O.K.

How Many ZZZs?

Some girls need more sleep than others. Most girls your age need about nine hours of sleep a night. While your body is growing and changing, you may need even more. Aim to get the same amount of sleep each night, no matter what day of the week it is or what time of year.

Sleep Troubles

Do you dread going to bed? Is nighttime a nightmare for you? If so, you're not alone. Lots of girls have problems that creep into their sleep.

Bed-Wetting

Wetting the bed is a condition that doctors call *enuresis* (en-yer-EE-sis), and it's much more common than you might think. Enuresis usually occurs when a girl's bladder is too small to hold all of the urine her body produces in the night. If the girl doesn't wake up in time to go to the bathroom, she wets the bed. The good news is that almost every girl with this condition outgrows it eventually. In the meantime, if you're struggling with enuresis, talk to your doctor. There are several treatments you can try—from alarms that help you wake up, to nasal sprays that decrease the amount of urine your body produces.

Insomnia

"I've got *insomnia*" is a fancy way of saying "I can't sleep." Insomnia is often caused by having a lot on your mind. You may be so excited or worried about something that you can't stop thinking about it. Insomnia can also be caused by caffeine and other chemicals in certain foods and medicines. Almost everyone has insomnia once in a while, but if you find yourself wide-awake night after night, talk to a parent or your doctor. In the meantime, try this relaxation trick. Close your eyes and lie on your back. Then relax your feet, relax your legs, and keep going until you've relaxed *every* muscle in your body. From head to toe, you'll be ready to go—straight to sleep, that is!

To unwind your mind, try listening to relaxing music or to recordings of soothing sounds from nature.

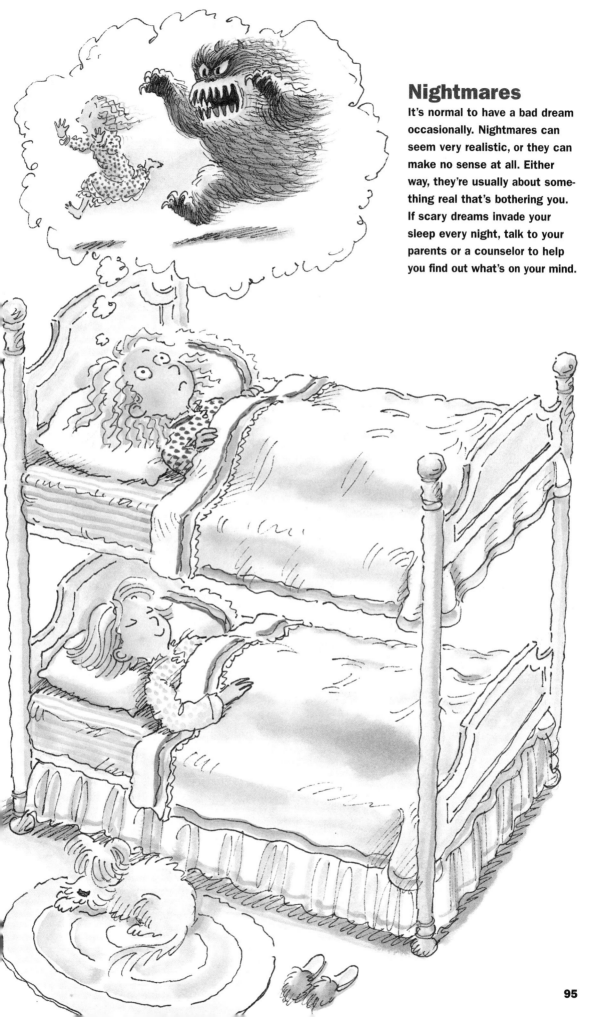

Nightmares

It's normal to have a bad dream occasionally. Nightmares can seem very realistic, or they can make no sense at all. Either way, they're usually about something real that's bothering you. If scary dreams invade your sleep every night, talk to your parents or a counselor to help you find out what's on your mind.

Body Talk

It's hard to feel perky in the A.M. when you've got **sleep** problems that plague you in the P.M.!

Too Worried to Sleep

I have trouble sleeping. I try reading before bed and much more. My parents are getting a divorce, but I don't like thinking about it. It hurts! Do you think deep in my mind I think about the divorce and it's keeping me up?

Hurt & Sleepy

Emotional upset and anxiety can definitely cause sleepless nights. Of course you feel scared and sad about your parents' divorce—any girl would. But when your daytime worries start to haunt you at bedtime, you need to do more than toss and turn. You need to get help. Talk to your parents, a teacher, a counselor, or another adult you trust about how much you're hurting. It's hard to have sweet dreams when you've got a heavy heart.

Security Blanket

I am 11 years old and I still sleep with a "blankie." I know a lot of girls do, but definitely not as old as me! Every time I go to a friend's to sleep over, she says stuff like, "Did you bring your security blanket?" and then laughs her head off.

Still sleeping with a "blankie"

Have you considered taking just a piece of your bedtime buddy with you? Cut off a teeny corner of your blanket and pin it inside your sleeping bag—a secret place that only you know about. Or, if you can't bear to cut up your blanket, maybe you can laugh along with your friend. When she asks about the blanket, say with a smile, "You know me, I never leave home without it!" And don't worry, you'll give up your blanket when you're ready.

Bed Wetter

I'm almost 12 and I still wet my bed. My best friend doesn't know and keeps inviting me to slumber parties. She feels sad when I say I can't go. I would really like to sleep over to make my friend happy, but how can I do it without getting embarrassed?

Ashamed

Keeping your bed-wetting a secret only adds to the feeling that it's something shameful—and it's not. If your friend is kind and caring, you may find there's relief in telling her the truth. You can still enjoy sleepovers with your friend by inviting her to your house. If she's having a party, ask if you can go to the first half of the party and have your parents pick you up before bedtime. You'll get to share in most of the fun. You're sure to outgrow bed-wetting eventually. But in the meantime, talk to your doctor about solutions.

Night Fright

I'm afraid of the dark and I can't sleep. What should I do?

afraid

For starters, you need to figure out exactly what it is about the dark that frightens you. Once you've identified what triggers your fright, ask your parents to help you brainstorm ways to banish your fears. Are there things in the room that scare you, such as the dark closet, the curtains flapping in the window, or other objects that cast scary shadows? Try placing a nightlight in your room so that you can see in all of the dark corners. Is it night noises that give you the heebie-jeebies? Investigate the source of the spooky sounds in the light of day. Once you know that "creak-creak" is coming from the furnace and not from phantoms, you're sure to rest easier.

The Girl Inside

Taking care of your **feelings** is just as important as taking care of your body. Find out what to do when oceans of emotions are washing over you, and get tips for **talking it out** with family and friends. Finally, as you get ready to move forward into the future, take a moment to stop and celebrate **the whole you!**

Your Feelings

Mad one minute, sad the next? Feel like you're riding an emotional roller coaster? You're not going crazy, you're just growing up.

Ups and Downs

You already know that during puberty the outside of you will undergo big changes. But you might not be prepared for so many changes inside of you. During this time, it's normal to experience very strong emotions. Don't be surprised if your moods come and go and change like the weather. One minute you're feeling sunny, the next minute stormy. What's behind this flood of laughter and tears? Hormones! The same hormones that tell your body to wake up and grow can strongly affect your feelings, too.

New Directions

As you get older, it's natural for your interests to change. Some of the toys and games you used to love suddenly get pushed to the back of the closet. New interests may take their place. You may also begin to notice boys in a whole different way. That's perfectly OK. There's room in your life for lots of different interests, old and new.

It's normal for a growing girl to want a little privacy. Just make sure that when you shut the bedroom door, you don't shut out the people you love. Puberty can be a confusing time, but it doesn't need to be a lonely one. Now more than ever, you need the support of your family.

Hang On

It's easy to get caught up in the tide of what other girls are saying and doing. They may even put pressure on you to do as they do. But be careful. It's easy to get lost in the crowd and lose sight of what's right for you. If your friends are going crazy about movie stars and makeup and you'd rather be building a tree fort, don't just cave in and go with the flow. Listen to your heart and be true to you.

Time Out!

Temper tantrums are OK for two-year-olds, who don't know how to control their emotions. But tears and screaming won't get you what you want now that you're older. Part of growing up is learning how to express anger and frustration calmly, in a way that's fair to others.

"It's good to **talk** out problems with the people you have them with." *Ukiah*

Dealing with Feelings

"Forget it. You won't understand."

"You treat me like a baby!"

"I hate you!"

Your whole world is turned topsy-turvy and there's a tidal wave of emotion crashing around inside of you. You might feel angry, jealous, afraid, embarrassed, or just plain lost and confused. What do you do? If you're like many people, you take it out on the people closest to you. And the trouble with this is that sulky silences and angry outbursts build a wall between people. The wall doesn't go up overnight—it's built one brick at a time. A mean word here. A slammed door there. Before you know it there's a wall too high for either side to climb over. Don't let this happen to you. Instead of building walls, build bridges by learning to say how you feel in a healthy, helpful way.

Cooling Down

Before you can talk about your feelings, you need to have a calm head. Take a few deep breaths. Take a walk. Take a bath. Write in your journal. Cuddle the dog. Blow off steam, and you'll be less likely to say or do something that you'll regret later. Once you've cooled down, you're ready to talk.

Talking It Out

Telling people how you feel, honestly and calmly, can bring you closer. It shows you trust them with your feelings. And you open the door for them to share their feelings with you. Besides, talking to others can help you sort out feelings that are confusing you. You need to be able to share anger, fear, and sadness—as well as excitement and happiness—to get the support you need during this challenging time.

Making It Better

Anger can be helpful when it leads to change. For that to happen, you need to try to explain how you feel. Follow these steps to say what's on your mind:

1 Describe exactly what made you angry. "Mom, it made me mad when you said I couldn't have a new swimsuit, right off the bat, without even listening to my reasons for wanting one."

2 Tell how it made you feel. "I felt like you didn't care about my feelings."

3 Try to agree on a way to handle things in the future. "Next time, let's hear each other out *before* deciding. Maybe together we'll think of a solution that will make us both happy."

The Whole You

Always remember there's more—much more—to you than your body. It's your head, your heart, and your spirit, too, that add up to make YOU.

Your eyes have a unique way of **seeing** the world.

Your head is abuzz with creative ideas, hopes, and **dreams.**

Your ears **listen** to other points of view.

Your voice confidently **expresses** your thoughts and feelings.

Your arms are always ready to **reach** out to others.

Your heart is full of **kindness.**

Your legs **stand up** for what's right.

Your feet are ready to **move ahead** to a bright future!